La lisière **au bord** ***le mur***

la séparation **au bout** la frontière la ligne de démarcation

à la fin la limite **la bordure**

de l'autre côté *à l'extrémité*

T0160866

La lisière **au bord** ***le mur***

la séparation **au bout** la frontière la ligne de démarcation

à la fin la limite **la bordure**

de l'autre côté *à l'extrémité*

Traverser *passer* franchir essayer **rallier**

rejoindre venir se rendre *se faufiler* **s'effacer**

transiter *changer* **disparaître** ***marcher*** s'en aller

se glisser **fuir** laisser *quitter* tenter

Traverser *passer* franchir essayer **rallier**

rejoindre venir se rendre *se faufiler* **s'effacer**

transiter *changer* **disparaître** ***marcher*** s'en aller

se glisser **fuir** laisser *quitter* tenter

but it's a long way

ATROX
that which cannot be eaten
:
an occasional series of works
published by Nightboat Books

but it's a long way

frédérique guétat-liviani
translated by nathanaël

Nightboat Books
New York

Copyright © 2017 by Frédérique Guétat-Liviani
English Translation Copyright © 2018 by Nathanaël
All rights reserved
Printed in the United States of America

mais ça fait loin was first published in 2017 in a portfolio of works under the title *la porte rouge* and jointly published by Fidel Anthelme X (Marseille) and L'Antre Lieux (Avignon). *la porte rouge* is comprised of texts by Anne Vuagnoux, Julien Blaine, Sarah Kéryna, Frédérique Guétat-Liviani and Liliane Giraudon.

ISBN: 978-1-937658-81-6

Design and typesetting by Kit Schluter

Collages by Frédérique Guétat-Liviani

Cataloging-in-publication data is available
from the Library of Congress

Distributed by the University Press of New England
One Court Street
Lebanon, NH 03766
www.upne.com

Nightboat Books
New York
www.nightboat.org

contents

7 | but it's a long way

43 | notes on the text

45 | mais ça fait loin

81 | contours and conditions of but it's a long way: an interview with Frédérique Guétat-Liviani

but it's a long way

a departure a departure of friends anonymous ones we can't
go back again it's been crossed we tried everything to break the silence
it's also the beliefs a beyond where the loved ones will come
help us the communion with them to find the disappeared
there are prayers these are gestures speaking yet there's a wall
words sometimes they're walls with those prayers we move beyond them

in the same language we all have a different definition of the same word
language locks us inside the words not love yes
there're people working to bring them down the walls
those who build them aren't very many but strong

us too when we're tired when we haven't slept well
we build them walls we shut ourselves inside them
10 on the news they speak of refugees i can't watch i'm too
disturbed they're fleeing their country the refugees they're fleeing suffering
they find themselves behind barbed wire i can't watch
i don't pray often it's rare that i pray
when i see images like that i pray right away it's immediate
i think i can do that pray

my mother she was a good person
the walls make me think of autism too
i worked at montfavet autistics are people who have so
much suffering it prevents them from reincarnating

reincarnation it's become obvious to me when i was 14 years old
it was hard to work there hard to feel oneself powerless
one brought what one could every day
some carers they were like angels but not all

i didn't build a wall to protect myself
we need sun but not the sun that burns us
when i was small i lived in the neighborhood at 20 i left
i was a dreamer i came back to live here

i came to france the suburbs in 1964 i
worked in construction before construction for 4 or 5 months

in agriculture i was born in morocco in rabah
it's the period of de gaulle houses cars
shops it's wide open now it's closed
the borders closed there's no more trust
in morocco i am no longer at home i'll go back in a box
now i am retired i stay home
between the old and the young there is a border

16 years in champfleury 12 years there 4 years there the neighborhood it's
good but the people i don't get on well with
the people who don't speak kindly my son is gentle he cries
the others hit him here i arrived young with my
husband we couldn't find a house we found a garage

for 3 months we slept in the garage i was pregnant after we found
a h.l.m. it's hard for me to talk about it that's where mom
she died dad lives here all alone i'm the eldest i was born
in france in 77 the following year we went back to live in
algeria i'm the only one with french papers
papers are a border between brothers and sisters
what i'd really like is to move but the cost of rent
it's too high that too is a border

it's hard to break them the walls what can we do
there are conflicts sometimes it's for a plot of land
in africa the borders they are forgotten when it's
to judge a president and then later they are put back to prevent
people from crossing me it's for love that i left

i followed my love the shock here it's when
i went to church for the first time no one

came to sit next to me
now i go to another church
in the ivory coast when a muslim dies catholic men go
to his funeral when it's a catholic who dies the muslims
go to the church in france the laws poison things

i don't like for my son to disrespect the elders
in africa you say i made food for everyone so everyone
eats teaching your children to do the dishes it's not
exploitation it's transmission

i live back there for 14 years no 15 since i am 15 years old
the projects for people it's synonymous with scum
that's why people don't want to come there's scum
everywhere it's education whether you're from a neighborhood or a village
it's education maybe people could be brought here to show
them we're not like that

in my section there are spaniards moroccans
algerians french people for 11 years i've been living in this section
we don't have problems among us before i was in
the other building it was the same i'm from morocco the center of morocco

when i said good-bye to my parents in front of the door to the house
there i crossed it the border my children their language it's french
now i think in both languages i count in french
even in my head later between my children and my parents
there will be another border it will be language

it's because of the fence water passes through the fence it makes a shadow
and it makes sun water it isn't hard it can pass

through the fence there are men in the water who die after
they won't die anymore they will live

people flee they're looking for peace but where they come from there is
unemployment poverty if it were possible to save someone
to open the door to close it again against the danger before
there were no borders no passports no papers
i arrived i was 23 i was too timid i didn't speak
after i spoke openly as though i were crossing the border

my father he crossed it the border in 37
to escape franco he had brothers in algeria he went there
he learned arabic my mother she only spoke spanish
they died i was small 6 years old i was placed in the orphanage
in avignon after i was called up in algeria it was war
but since i was a breadwinner yes for my sister breadwinner
i soon came back demobilized in marseille i worked as a
driver i met a girl from marseille when she got pregnant
we had to get married i wasn't of age i was a ward of the nation we
asked for a permit from the president of the republic

later with my sister we went to spain to almeria to see if
our grandfather's sheepfold was still there we were watched
by the civic guard we were told there's nothing left for the children
of republicans my own children have never been to spain

every morning i go to the community center to make coffee
to meet people before that i took care of collecting food
18 it was for soup kitchens i also go to the secours populaire to
collect school supplies at the start of the school year and the rest of the time
for food and baby care the border between wealthy
people and poor people that's the one i look after
even if i didn't know them it's what i have left
of the political awareness of my parents

it's language french it's been 10 months actually before i learned
french but after i was and i forgot french
i stayed 14 years in my children were born in we left

because of the crisis no more work for my husband my husband was born in
he always lived in but he speaks french well because he goes out
with friends me i stay home it's harder to
learn to speak my nationality it allows me to live in france
i want to speak french i want to work i live there
on the 7th floor the elevator is broken it's been 3 months but here
i feel good where i was before the people weren't kind
i lived with family really i'm better off here next
week i'm going back to see my brother don't put
the names of places and people to avoid my being recognized

you can't cross because of the wall otherwise you'll run into it
there on the other hand you can cross there's a hole in a wall and there a fence

you climb the fence but if you don't know how to climb what do you do
when there is a river you can make a bridge everyone
can go to the other side and walk

school it is at the edge of our neighborhoods
we meet less often when places are not bordering
it's been 6 years that i've been living in the neighborhood there were some tense
periods and then the border became a bit diluted

i've been working at the collège for 7 years i teach technology
i try to give tools to the children they are handicapped by the
poverty of their vocabulary it's a real handicap but what's most important
for me is to prove to them that they are capable of making it

when the new gymnasium was built someone wrote on the wall
of the building full of mistakes *i wanna work at citi hull*
at the bus stop another one wrote *here it's the laaw of silence* because
in this zone there is another law the 2 a's of *laaw* must be for that

i live on the border between monclar and champfleury i am
a border dweller by birth born in algeria on the moroccan border
my grandparents were from morocco but us we felt algerian
my first name my parents gave it to me in homage to the algerian
president we were run out in 75 the army woke us at 4 in the morning
we were allowed to take a blanket with us the women on one truck
with the children the men on another truck

in algeria i wasn't schooled i was with the animals
it was good my grandparents looked after me i collected the almonds
i took care of the chicken coop repatriated to morocco my parents schooled me
because of my first name the schoolmaster hit my fingers all
morning long with a palm branch in the afternoon i ran away

for 2 years we lived all 5 of us in a single room
it became impossible my father who worked in france
found a place to bring us here
they bought me shoes for the first time

my father was a farm worker his employer was a very good man
he was the mayor of the village without a title my sister today
is a town councilor in the same village

when we arrived it was the month of march i didn't know a word of french
i learned very quickly by repeating the words i heard
my brothers and sisters born in algeria were like me at school they always
wanted to be head of the class an invisible border turned
my young brothers born in france away from culture

i have an illness diabetes it's the illness of the in-between
one is never at the right place at the right time
my border-dweller illness

19 years in france 5 at monclar i come from teaz not far
from nador i left at age 14 with my parents
i was happy to leave we arrived at porto vecchio
it's expensive life in corsica my husband found work here
my children all 3 they were born here my life is here

i come from the same village as najat in algeria i arrived in
france 2 years ago i didn't speak any french at all if i speak
french well it's thanks to najat my father speaks french well
because his mother she was born in france then she got married to
an algerian over there my father he was born in algeria
he got married to my mother in algeria also they left
for the south in ghardaïa what was i saying oh yes

in ghardaïa it wasn't working out there were family problems so
we left we settled in algiers but we had to leave again because
my father's mother she fell ill my little brother was born there
and after we left again for algiers it wasn't working out again
that's why we filled out the papers my mother said got to go far away

and we arrived in avignon
we moved in to my uncle's for 2 months not even
24 but with the family it still wasn't going well my father found work
and an apartment it's there on the 9th floor a two-room flat
i sleep with my big sister we are 4 children
my mother is pregnant with the baby that will make 5
my big sister is 19 my little brother is 8 the youngest is 3 that's her

within a year my grandmother she called she said here we are
so we went to pick up my grandfather and my grandmother at marignane
they moved in to my uncle's but another day my grandmother
called my father again come get us your brother wants to hit your father
that's when they came to live with us it caused trouble with my uncle
my grandfather became sick when he was 70

my father right now he is in algeria to bury my
grandfather the timing is bad my father had an accident at work
when my grandfather got sick it's my father who looked after him
to the end he changed him he washed him he cared for him

i was afraid of coming to france but i found najat i found a friend
now i would be afraid to leave to leave her here i would just like
to travel yes travel and come back to her

they can pass there is a door but it's closed
locked shut you can make a hole in the wall on the other side
of the wall there is a house and a garden

you have to be aware of misery misery brings
anger revolt if everyone stays locked inside himself if everyone has
26 his own personal wall it's no good it has to be destroyed this wall
the demarcation line is the one that prevents from going elsewhere
it's been 40 years since i've been living in the neighborhood i am a member of
the association of renters we fought a lot against rent increases
to bring the expenses down for rat control there are believers
non-believers we have to come together to fight right now we
are circulating a petition for the replacement
of the wastewater column crossing the border this idea
my father passed it on to me picked up by the s.t.o he escaped 4 times
denounced by a schoolmate he joined the f.f.i my grandfather
he was a socialist my father after the war he became a firefighter
his hatred of collaborators he held on to it for a long time

life is good outside but with the children it's
hard life is expensive almost 10 years since i've been
here across from the school there is some concern with the school but

the place where i live is calm at school there are children
and moms who say swear words in front of the others i have 2 children
my daughter is 7 years old my son is 4 before i was at brive la gaillarde and
before that in morocco i came here at age 16 i only spoke arabic french
i learned it here with my children i only speak in french
they understand arabic but they don't know how to speak it with my husband
we speak 3 languages we are berber in morocco at home
we spoke berber at school we spoke arabic

my parents when they decided to leave me i was crying
we took the car two days of travel we crossed spain
28 we were 5 children another one was born later 7 in the van
my father was already working in france he was working at the factory now
he is retired he returned to live in morocco but he comes back to see us
all the time when they are older i will teach
my children to write in arabic i didn't want to leave morocco
but now it's hard to go back
i go there in the winter when it's less hot my husband it's been 8 years
since he doesn't go anymore he works at the factory at the food processing plant

i'm looking for work i can't find any i have the permit but no car
as a result i stay home otherwise it causes trouble with
the neighbors i have a friend in châteaurenard she comes
to the house every friday she doesn't have children mine

are hers when i'm old i'll do like my father
i'll live between both countries i need both

every summer i cross spain the economic crisis there
it's very serious i arrived here i was 8 years old at school in
morocco i had learned several words of french but at home
we spoke arabic before leaving my parents warned me
i said good-bye to everyone my father was an electrician
he had left before us he was already working here now my father he's retired

when i arrived at school i was made fun of but i made myself
a friend he gave me candies we didn't leave one another after that
at first both of us we spoke together in sign language
at home we spoke arabic at his home turkish together in french
after 2 months i spoke well it's been 9 years now
last year he returned to live in turkey we grew up
like brothers i miss him i would like to see him again

i want to be a general practitioner it's thanks to my sister that i want
to be a doctor my sister all this time she's wanted to be a doctor

my cousins they were born in france when they go to morocco they are laughed at
my little brother too was born here among brothers and sisters
we speak french with my mother arabic with my father both
i have good grades at school the others are jealous because
i'm a bledard school is the survival of the fittest every man for himself
i do ground fighting i wear the colors of france i have
dual citizenship i loathe soccer running after a ball
earning millions a dog can do that other people
who do extraordinary things no one's gonna talk about it

one evening in morocco i was a child i got lost a homeless person
took me in what he had earned begging that day he spent it to
give me food the next day he found my house he took me
back to my father now i live at la reine jeanne
2 days ago a man died of old age we were all there to say good-bye to him

my little brother i let him play outside in the neighborhood it's the only place
where i'm not worried the dealers themselves they want
to protect us so we don't become like them they look out for us
in the summer when we go away they watch the houses since they were
born they've lived outside no one to take care of them
when they grow up they regret it they say so i find it sad

sometimes there are even wars because of the separations
there are also the borders you can't see between arabs and
the racist french it comes from generalization the terrorists
they say you have to kill in the name of islam so people believe
all muslims are like that but there's also racism
on the part of maghrebians toward others

i am albanian i'm 14 years old i'm muslim it doesn't show
when i'm alone people don't give me funny looks for example
at the supermarket checkout when i'm not buying much
i ask if i can go ahead of the full shopping carts i'm told yes
but when i'm with my aunt she wears a scarf
they don't let us pass the eyes are cold i think that
religion it's something personal it shouldn't trace borders
albanians from kossovo suffered a lot my older sister who's 17
she doesn't wear the veil she has plenty of time i feel french
with origins from elsewhere when i was small we moved
a lot we were never able to stop worrying and then
when we learned that my aunt was here we came

i'm a bit pessimistic for the future there will be more and more
refugees maybe there will be a 3rd world war i'm afraid
of the future now in kossovo a false calm reigns the other time
there was a match between albania and serbia a toy flew over the stadium
a small remote control helicopter with an albanian flag the flag fell
onto the pitch a serbian tore up the flag so the albanians
fought against the serbians my dream would be to create
a movement to help people to open their eyes being kind
being mean it's a choice it has nothing to do with origins

in kossovo when you come from the same village everyone has the same name
even if we're not related i find that beautiful
we're not required to be from the same family to feel solidarity

it's an end the end of something the beginning of something else
there is another beginning the other day we were in chlef we went
to maghnia at the border where people exchange
goods with those on the other side the houses had
hot colors we went on a whim just to see

i have family in morocco i've never seen them on mom's side
we are from chlef and algiers from bab-el-oued on dad's side
from oujda they are algerians but also moroccans and also catalans my
great-grandfather he came from barcelona my great-aunt she lives in
barcelona we speak on the telephone i speak arabic and french
i'm learning english and spanish i'm quite good at spanish

my ancestors are here my great-grandfather he arrived in marseille
he settled down in avignon to work my great grandfather was born
in algeria he came here in 63 my dad was born here
mom in chlef the first time she came she was 6 months old
she left she came back when she was 4 she left again she came back at 19
my parents speak together in the 2 languages they speak to me in the 2 languages
my first language is french then the arabic language got
the upper hand now it's balanced out again i got back yesterday
from algeria it was too hot it had been 3 years since i hadn't been back

in marseille too i have family in la castellane in consolat in la belle de mai
here in the area i have my 2 grandmothers in chlef there's a whole area
it's just my family i'd really like to put here all the people i like in chlef
and in chlef all the people that i like here i'm a bit torn over there
i like the landscapes the countryside the chickens the cows the sheep

to tell you the truth i prefer marseille to avignon but i also like avignon
because avignon is my city i feel good at monclar

at the end of every story there is a new story me
i feel like i grew up too fast

we hate one another because we don't speak the same language
sometimes we can hate one another because of the attacks
we don't know each other well when we don't speak the same language
the rivers the seas they're borders in truth
i'd like to go to china i'd like to go to peking
i go to mayotte from time to time but it's a long way

there are bridges i already crossed the border of belgium
and the border of england my family is in france
in england in algeria i was born in avignon at urbain 5
those on my mother's side live in england my mother she is originally from
there but i don't talk to her much in class i don't have good grades
in english on the other hand when i speak with the english i can manage
when playing *clash of clan* then i manage well

once i went to england but it's expensive you're better off living
in dunkerque that way you can work during the day go home at night
on my father-in-law's side i have family in algeria i quite like avignon
but i prefer marseille because in marseille
there is a subway with car wheels

the first day when you go to school you cross a border
after it's everyday life later i'd really like

to cross the borders of america go all over

sometimes borders are between friends when we argue
it blocks us we withdraw instead of moving forward

with adults the border it's the secrets they keep
for example when someone dies and also when
they don't want to say what gift they're going to give us
age memory words that you don't know
that's what it is their border

an argument that could separate us
i was born in mayotte i've been here for 3 months i'm in 8th grade
i left my little sister my little brother my father i left with my mother
my other little brother he is in marseille at my uncle's
my dream was to see the eiffel tower for real but the trip was very very
long when we arrived in paris it was a friend of my mother's who
brought us as far as the subway to go to the station to take the train i couldn't
see the eiffel tower i would like to return to paris to see it
once in marseille we spent the day i was exhausted
completely exhausted then we left by car again to go to my aunt's
mom's sister here at monclar while waiting to find accommodation

it hurts me to have left the twins on the 16th they turned 9
so far i still haven't made any friends there are those
who make fun because for my age i'm small
the problem is that over there there were too many thugs for example if
you were from the city called cavani the rivals those from m'gombani
they would come they'd slaughter you that's why my mother
she said we had to leave i'm a bit worried for my father
my brother and my sister the ones who stayed

here it's calm we're looking for a house if we don't find one we'll go to marseille
or paris i'd rather live in a calm city

a peaceful city like avignon

the french language here it runs in the veins the people who live far away
they tell themselves we don't speak well we have to learn to speak well
the people here don't realize that it runs in their veins

i'd like to study medicine if i can't i'll join the army
in mayotte i reread my notebooks at night in the morning i got up
at 5 o'clock to review a bit i didn't like koranic school
but what's good is that i learned to read arabic this year between
spanish and arabic i chose spanish to know a new language

right now i often have headaches noise gives me a headache when i was in mayotte the 6th grade classes were named after flowers the 7th after authors the 8th i can't remember in 9th grade names of european capitals since i was in 7th grade rousseau i looked the name up on the internet i read a bunch of things on rousseau on the education of children i even know that his first name was jean-jacques abdelsam michel-françois michel najat

rabiâa leïla ensar mireille souhail

odile chloé samira boumedienne lucas

najat s nadia hayat nasser

kassym 4 years old samaar 7 years old kaïna 7 and a half fakri 9 and a half

july 11 16 july 12 16 july 26 16 july 27 16

granges d'orel *champfleury* *granges d'orel* *champfleury*

monclar *monclar*

late morning *late afternoon* *day's end*

frédérique guétat-liviani october 16 saint-ruf

notes on the text

Bledard, sometimes spelled with an acute accent on the e (é), broadly designates a person from the Maghreb, though it can specifically denote an immigrant to France of North African origin. Bledard can be negatively connoted and used as an insult. Derived from bled, a familiar term used in the Maghreb to denote a town, a village, a county.

H.L.M. —*habitation à loyer modéré*— refers to public or private rent-controlled housing in France.

F.F.I. —*Les forces françaises de l'intérieur* (French forces of the interior)— designates the consolidation, under this name, of the principal military resistance groups in WWII, beginning in December 1943. The group would eventually be dissolved by de Gaulle and its members absorbed into the military. (Source: *Dictionnaire historique de la résistance*, Robert Laffont, 2006)

Marignane is the old name of the Marseille Provence airport.

Montfavet is a mental health hospital located in Avignon.

Secours populaire is a French popular relief organization dedicated to fighting poverty and discrimination.

S.T.O. —*Le service de travail obligatoire* (compulsory work service)— refers to a series of laws implemented in 1942-1943 by the Vichy regime at the request of the occupying German authorities, and resulting in the forced dispatch of several hundred thousand French people to feed the Nazi labor force. France was the only European country to force its citizens into collaboration. (Source: *Encyclopaedia Universalis*)

mais ça fait loin

un départ un départ d'amis d'anonymes on pourra plus
revenir en arrière c'est franchi on a tout tenté pour casser le silence
c'est aussi les croyances un au-delà où les aimés vont venir
nous aider la communion avec eux pour retrouver les disparus
il y a les prières ce sont des gestes des paroles pourtant y'a un mur
les mots des fois c'est des murs avec ces prières-là on passe par-dessus

dans la même langue on a tous une définition différente du même mot
le langage ça nous enferme dans les mots pas l'amour oui
y'a des gens qui œuvrent pour les faire tomber les murs
ceux qui les construisent sont pas nombreux mais forts

nous aussi quand on est fatigué quand on a mal dormi
on en construit des murs on s'enferme dedans
aux actualités ils parlent des réfugiés je peux pas regarder je suis trop
perturbée ils fuient leur pays les réfugiés ils fuient la souffrance
ils se retrouvent derrière des barbelés je peux pas regarder
je prie pas souvent c'est rare que je prie
quand je vois des images comme ça je prie tout de suite c'est instantané
je crois que je peux faire ça prier

ma mère c'était quelqu'un de bien
les murs me font penser à l'autisme aussi
j'ai travaillé à montfavet les autistes ce sont des gens qui ont tant
de souffrance ça les empêche de se réincarner

la réincarnation c'est devenu évident pour moi quand j'ai eu 14 ans
c'était difficile de travailler là difficile de se sentir impuissant
on apportait ce qu'on pouvait au quotidien
certains soignants ils étaient comme des anges mais pas tous

j'ai pas construit de mur pour me protéger
on a besoin du soleil mais pas du soleil qui nous brûle
petite je vivais dans le quartier à 20 ans je suis partie j'étais rêveuse
je suis revenue vivre ici

j'arrive en france en banlieue en 1964 je
travaille dans le bâtiment avant le bâtiment pendant 4 ou 5 mois

dans l'agriculture je nais au maroc à rabah
c'est l'époque de de gaulle les maisons les voitures
les magasins c'est tout ouvert maintenant c'est fermé
les frontières c'est fermé il y a plus la confiance
au maroc je suis plus chez moi j'y retournerai dans la boîte
maintenant je suis à la retraite je reste à la maison
entre les vieux et les jeunes il y a la frontière

16 ans à champfleury 12 ans là 4 ans là le quartier il est
bien mais les gens je m'entends pas bien avec
les gens qui parlent pas gentiment mon fils est doux il pleure
les autres le frappent ici je suis arrivée jeune avec mon
mari on n'a pas trouvé de maison on a trouvé un garage

pendant 3 mois on a dormi dans le garage j'étais enceinte après on a
trouvé un h.l.m. j'ai du mal à parler de ça c'est là que maman
elle est morte papa vit tout seul ici je suis l'aînée je suis née
en france en 77 l'année suivante on est repartis vivre en
algérie je suis la seule à avoir les papiers français
les papiers c'est une frontière entre frères et sœurs
ce que j'aimerais bien c'est déménager mais le prix des loyers
c'est trop cher ça aussi c'est une frontière

c'est dur de les casser les murs qu'est-ce qu'on peut faire
il y a des conflits des fois c'est pour une parcelle
en afrique les frontières on les oublie quand c'est
pour juger un président et puis après on les remet pour empêcher
les gens de passer moi c'est par amour que je suis partie

j'ai suivi mon amour le choc ici c'est quand
je suis allée à l'église la première fois personne
n'est venu s'asseoir près de moi
maintenant je vais dans une autre église
en côte d'ivoire quand un musulman meurt les hommes catholiques vont
à son enterrement quand c'est un catholique qui meurt les musulmans
vont à l'église en france les lois enveniment les choses

je n'aime pas que mon fils manque de respect aux aînés
en afrique on dit j'ai cuisiné pour tout le monde alors tout le monde
en mange apprendre à faire la vaisselle à ses enfants c'est pas de
l'exploitation c'est de la transmission

j'habite derrière depuis 14 ans non 15 puisque j'ai 15 ans
les cités pour les gens c'est synonyme de racaille
c'est à cause de ça que les gens veulent pas venir les racailles y en a
partout c'est l'éducation qu'on soit d'un quartier ou d'un village
c'est l'éducation peut-être on pourrait faire venir les gens leur
montrer qu'on n'est pas comme ça

dans ma montée il y a des espagnols des marocains
des algériens des français ça fait 11 ans que j'habite la montée
on n'a pas de problèmes entre nous avant j'étais dans
l'autre bâtiment c'était pareil je suis du maroc du centre du maroc

quand j'ai dit au revoir à mes parents devant la porte de la maison
là je l'ai passée la frontière mes enfants leur langue c'est le français
maintenant je pense dans les 2 langues je compte en français
même dans ma tête plus tard entre mes enfants et mes parents
il y aura une autre frontière ce sera la langue

c'est à cause du grillage l'eau passe par le grillage ça fait de l'ombre
et ça fait du soleil l'eau elle est pas dure elle peut passer à
travers le grillage il y a des bonhommes dans l'eau qui meurent après
ils vont plus mourir ils vont vivre

les gens fuient ils cherchent la paix mais là où ils viennent il y a
le chômage la pauvreté si c'était possible de sauver quelqu'un
d'ouvrir la porte de la refermer sur le danger avant
il y avait pas de frontières pas de passeports pas de papiers
je suis arrivée j'avais 23 ans j'étais trop timide je parlais pas
après j'ai parlé franchement comme si je passais la frontière

mon père il l'a franchie lui la frontière en 37
pour fuir franco il avait des frères en algérie il est parti là-bas
il a appris l'arabe ma mère elle parlait que l'espagnol
ils sont morts j'étais petit 6 ans on m'a placé à l'orphelinat
d'avignon après j'ai été appelé en algérie c'était la guerre
mais comme j'étais soutien de famille oui pour ma sœur soutien de famille
je suis vite rentré démobilisé à marseille j'ai travaillé comme
chauffeur j'ai rencontré une fille une marseillaise quand elle a été enceinte
il a fallu qu'on se marie j'étais pas majeur j'étais pupille de la nation on a
demandé une autorisation au président de la république

plus tard avec ma sœur on est allés en espagne à almeria voir si
la bergerie de notre grand-père était encore là on était surveillés
par la garde civile on nous a dit il y a plus rien pour les enfants
des républicains mes enfants à moi ils sont jamais allés en espagne

tous les matins je vais au centre social préparer le café
pour rencontrer les gens avant je me suis occupé du ramassage alimentaire

c'était pour les restos du cœur je vais aussi au secours populaire pour le
ramassage des fournitures scolaires à la rentrée et le reste du temps
pour l'alimentation et le soin des bébés la frontière entre les gens
aisés et les gens pauvres c'est celle-là dont je m'occupe
même si je les ai pas connus c'est ce qui me reste
de la conscience politique de mes parents

c'est la langue le français ça fait 10 mois enfin avant j'ai appris
le français mais après j'étais et j'ai oublié le français
je suis restée 14 ans en mes enfants sont nés à on est partis

à cause de la crise plus de travail pour mon mari mon mari est né en
il a toujours vécu en mais il parle bien le français parce qu'il sort
avec des copains moi je reste à la maison c'est plus difficile pour
apprendre à parler ma nationalité elle me permet de vivre en france
je veux parler français je veux travailler j'habite là
au 7ème étage l'ascenseur est cassé ça fait 3 mois mais ici
je me sens bien où j'étais avant les gens étaient pas gentils
j'habitais avec la famille vraiment je suis mieux ici la semaine
prochaine j'y retourne pour voir mon frère il faudra pas mettre
les noms des endroits et des gens pour pas qu'on me reconnaisse

on peut pas passer à cause du mur sinon on va se cogner
là par contre on peut passer il y a un mur troué et là un grillage

on grimpe au grillage mais si on sait pas grimper qu'est-ce qu'on fait
quand il y a une rivière on peut faire un pont chacun
peut y aller de l'autre côté et marcher

l'école elle est à la limite de nos quartiers
on se rencontre moins quand les lieux sont pas frontaliers
ça fait 6 ans que j'habite le quartier il y a eu des périodes tendues
et puis la frontière s'est un peu diluée

je travaille au collège depuis 7 ans j'enseigne la technologie
j'essaie de donner des outils aux enfants ils sont handicapés par la
pauvreté de leur vocabulaire c'est un vrai handicap mais le plus important
pour moi c'est de leur prouver qu'ils sont capables d'y arriver

quand le nouveau gymnase a été construit quelqu'un a écrit sur le mur du bâtiment avec plein de fautes *je veu travaillé a la mairi* à l'arrêt de bus un autre a écrit *ici c'est la loii du silence* parce que dans cette zone il y a une autre loi les 2 *i de loii* ça doit être pour ça

je vis à la frontière entre monclar et champfleury je suis un frontalier de naissance né en algérie à la frontière marocaine mes grands-parents étaient du maroc mais nous on se sentait algériens mon prénom mes parents me l'ont donné en hommage au président algérien on a été chassés en 75 l'armée nous a réveillés à 4 heures du matin on a eu le droit d'emporter une couverture les femmes dans un camion avec les enfants les hommes dans un autre camion

en algérie j'étais pas scolarisé j'étais avec les bêtes j'étais bien mes grands-parents s'occupaient de moi je ramassais les amandes je m'occupais du poulailler rapatriés au maroc mes parents m'ont scolarisé à cause de mon prénom le maître d'école m'a tapé sur les doigts toute la matinée avec une branche de palmier l'après-midi je me suis enfui

pendant 2 ans on a vécu tous les 5 dans une seule pièce
c'était plus possible mon père qui travaillait en france

a trouvé un logement pour nous faire venir
on m'a acheté des chaussures pour la première fois

mon père était ouvrier agricole son employeur était un homme très bon
c'était le maire du village sans étiquette ma sœur aujourd'hui
est conseillère municipale dans le même village

quand on est arrivés c'était le mois de mars je savais pas un mot de français
j'ai appris très vite en répétant les mots que j'entendais
mes frères et sœurs nés en algérie étaient comme moi à l'école ils voulaient
toujours être les premiers une frontière invisible a détourné
de la culture mes jeunes frères nés en france

j'ai une maladie le diabète c'est la maladie de l'entre-deux
on n'est jamais au bon endroit au bon moment
ma maladie de frontalier

19 ans en france 5 à monclar je viens de teaz juste à côté
de nador je suis partie à 14 ans avec mes parents
j'étais contente de partir on est arrivés à porto vecchio
c'est cher la vie en corse mon mari a trouvé du travail ici
mes enfants les 3 ils sont nés ici ma vie elle est ici

je viens du même village que najat en algérie je suis arrivée en
france il y a 2 ans je parlais pas du tout français si je parle
bien français c'est grâce à najat mon père parle bien le français
parce que sa mère elle est née en france puis elle s'est mariée avec
un algérien là-bas mon père lui il est né en algérie
il s'est marié avec ma mère en algérie aussi ils sont partis
dans le sud à gardaïa qu'est-ce que je disais ah oui

à gardaïa ça marchait pas trop y avait des problèmes de famille alors
on est partis on s'est installés à alger mais il a fallu repartir parce que
la mère de mon père elle est tombée malade mon petit-frère est né là
et après on est repartis à alger ça n'allait encore pas
c'est pour ça qu'on a fait les papiers ma mère a dit faut partir loin

et on est arrivés à avignon
on s'est installés chez mon oncle pendant 2 mois même pas
mais avec la famille ça n'allait toujours pas mon père a trouvé du travail
et un appartement c'est là au 9ème étage un 2 pièces
je dors avec ma grande sœur on est 4 enfants
ma mère est enceinte avec le bébé ça fera 5
ma grande sœur a 19 ans mon petit frère a 8 ans la petite a 3 ans c'est elle

au bout d'un an ma grand-mère elle a téléphoné elle a dit on est là
alors on est allés chercher mon grand-père et ma grand-mère à marignane
ils se sont installés chez mon oncle mais un autre jour ma grand-mère
elle a encore appelé mon père viens nous chercher ton frère veut frapper ton père
c'est là qu'ils sont venus habiter chez nous ça a fait des histoires avec mon tonton
mon grand-père est tombé malade à 70 ans

mon père en ce moment il est en algérie pour enterrer mon grand-père ça tombe mal mon père a eu un accident au travail quand mon grand-père est tombé malade c'est mon père qui s'est occupé de lui jusqu'au bout il le changeait il le lavait il le soignait

j'avais peur de venir en france mais j'ai trouvé najat j'ai trouvé une amie maintenant j'aurais peur de m'en aller de la laisser ici j'aimerais juste voyager voilà voyager et revenir la retrouver

ils peuvent passer il y a une porte mais elle est fermée à clef on peut faire un trou dans le mur de l'autre côté du mur il y a une maison et un jardin

il faut en prendre conscience de la misère la misère amène
la colère la révolte si chacun reste enfermé en lui-même si chacun a
son mur personnel ça va pas il faut le détruire ce mur
la ligne de démarcation c'est elle qui empêche d'aller ailleurs
ça fait 40 ans que j'habite le quartier je fais partie de l'amicale
des locataires on a beaucoup lutté contre la hausse des loyers
pour faire baisser les charges pour faire dératiser il y a des croyants
des non-croyants on doit s'unir pour lutter en ce moment on
fait circuler une pétition pour le remplacement
de la colonne des eaux usées franchir la frontière cette idée
c'est mon père qui me l'a passée embarqué au s.t.o il s'est évadé 4 fois
dénoncé par un copain d'école il a rejoint les f.f.i mon grand-père
il était socialiste mon père après la guerre il est devenu pompier
la haine des collabos il l'a gardée longtemps

la vie est bien dehors mais avec les enfants c'est
difficile la vie est chère presque 10 ans que je suis là
en face de l'école il y a un peu de souci avec l'école mais

la place où j'habite c'est calme à l'école il y a des enfants
et des mamans qui disent des gros mots devant les autres j'ai 2 enfants
ma fille a 7 ans mon fils a 4 ans avant j'étais à brive la gaillarde et
avant au maroc je suis venue à 16 ans je parlais qu'arabe le français
je l'ai appris ici avec mes enfants je parle qu'en français
ils comprennent l'arabe mais ils savent pas le parler avec mon mari
on parle 3 langues on est berbères au maroc à la maison
on parlait berbère à l'école on parlait arabe

mes parents quand ils ont décidé de partir moi je pleurais
on a pris la voiture deux jours de voyage on a traversé l'espagne
on était 5 enfants un autre est né plus tard 7 dans la fourgonnette
mon père travaillait déjà en france il travaillait à l'usine maintenant
il est à la retraite il est retourné vivre au maroc mais il revient nous voir
tout le temps quand ils seront plus grands j'apprendrai
à écrire l'arabe à mes enfants je voulais pas quitter le maroc
mais maintenant c'est dur d'y retourner
j'y vais en hiver quand il fait moins chaud mon mari ça fait 8 ans
qu'il y va plus il travaille à l'usine à l'usine agroalimentaire

je cherche du travail je trouve pas j'ai le permis mais pas de voiture
du coup je reste à la maison sinon ça fait des histoires avec
les voisines j'ai une amie à châteaurenard elle vient
à la maison tous les vendredis elle a pas d'enfants les miens

c'est les siens quand je vieillirai je ferai comme mon père
je vivrai entre les 2 pays j'ai besoin des 2

tous les étés je traverse l'espagne la crise économique là-bas
elle est très grave je suis arrivé ici j'avais 8 ans à l'école au
maroc j'avais appris quelques mots de français mais à la maison
on parlait arabe avant de partir mes parents m'ont prévenu
j'ai dit au revoir à tout le monde mon père était électricien
il était parti avant nous il travaillait déjà ici mon père maintenant il est retraité

quand je suis arrivé à l'école on s'est moqué de moi mais je me suis fait
un ami il m'a donné des bonbons on s'est plus quittés
au début tous les 2 on se parlait la langue des signes
chez moi on parlait arabe chez lui turc ensemble le français
au bout de 2 mois je parlais bien ça fait 9 ans maintenant
l'année dernière il est retourné vivre en turquie on a grandi
comme des frères il me manque je voudrais le revoir

je veux être généraliste c'est ma sœur qui m'a donné envie
d'être médecin ma sœur depuis tout le temps elle veut être médecin
mes cousins ils sont nés en france quand ils vont au maroc on se moque d'eux
mon petit frère aussi est né ici entre frères et sœurs
on parle français avec ma mère l'arabe avec mon père les 2
j'ai de bons résultats scolaires les autres sont jaloux parce que
je suis un bledard l'école c'est la loi du plus fort chacun pour soi
je fais du combat au sol je porte les couleurs de la france j'ai la
double nationalité je déteste le foot courir derrière un ballon
gagner des millions un chien peut le faire d'autres gens qui
font des choses extraordinaires personne va en parler

un soir au maroc j'étais enfant je me suis perdu un s.d.f
m'a recueilli ce qu'il avait gagné en mendiant la journée il l'a dépensé pour
me donner à manger le lendemain il a retrouvé ma maison il m'a
ramené chez mon père maintenant j'habite à la reine jeanne
il y a 2 jours un homme est mort de vieillesse on était tous là pour lui dire au revoir

mon petit frère je le laisse jouer dehors dans le quartier il y a que là
que je suis pas inquiet les dealers eux-mêmes ils veulent nous
protéger pour qu'on devienne pas comme eux ils font attention à nous
l'été quand on part ils surveillent les maisons depuis qu'ils sont
nés ils ont vécu dehors personne pour s'occuper d'eux
quand ils sont grands ils regrettent ils le disent je trouve ça triste

des fois il y a même des guerres à cause des séparations
il y a aussi les frontières qui se voient pas entre les arabes et
les français racistes ça vient de la généralisation les terroristes
ils disent qu'il faut tuer au nom de l'islam alors on croit
que tous les musulmans sont comme ça mais y'a aussi du racisme
de la part des maghrébins vis-à-vis des autres

je suis albanais j'ai 14 ans je suis musulman ça se voit pas
quand je suis seul les gens me regardent pas de travers par exemple
à la caisse du supermarché quand je prends pas grand-chose
je demande si je peux passer devant les caddies remplis on me dit oui
mais quand je suis avec ma tante elle porte un foulard
on nous laisse pas passer les regards sont froids je crois que
la religion c'est un truc personnel ça doit pas tracer des frontières
les albanais du kossovo ont beaucoup souffert ma grande sœur de 17 ans
elle porte pas le voile elle a bien le temps je me sens français
avec des origines d'ailleurs quand j'étais petit on a
beaucoup déménagé on n'arrivait jamais à se tranquilliser et puis
quand on a appris que ma tante était là on est venus

je suis un peu pessimiste pour l'avenir il y aura de plus en plus de réfugiés peut-être qu'il y aura une 3ème guerre mondiale j'ai peur de l'avenir maintenant au kossovo le faux calme règne l'autre fois y'a eu un match albanie serbie un jouet a survolé le stade un petit hélicoptère téléguidé avec un drapeau albanais le drapeau est tombé sur le terrain un serbe a déchiré le drapeau alors les albanais se sont battus contre les serbes mon rêve ce serait de créer un mouvement pour aider les gens à ouvrir les yeux être gentil être méchant c'est un choix ça n'a rien à voir avec les origines

au kossovo quand on vient du même village on porte tous le même nom même si on n'est pas apparentés je trouve ça beau on n'est pas obligés d'être de la même famille pour être solidaires

c'est une fin la fin de quelque chose le début d'autre chose
il y a un autre début l'autre jour on était à chlef on est

partis à maghnia à la frontière là où les gens échangent
des marchandises avec ceux de l'autre côté les maisons avaient
des couleurs chaudes on y est allés comme ça juste pour voir

j'ai de la famille au maroc je l'ai jamais vue du côté de maman
on est de chlef et d'alger de bab-el-oued du côté de papa
d'oujda ils sont algériens mais aussi marocains et aussi catalans mon
arrière-grand-père il venait de barcelone ma grand-tante elle habite à
barcelone on se parle au téléphone je parle arabe et français
j'apprends l'anglais et l'espagnol je suis plutôt forte en espagnol

mes ancêtres sont ici mon arrière-grand-père il est arrivé à marseille
il s'est installé à avignon pour travailler mon grand-père est né
en algérie il est venu ici en 63 mon papa est né ici
maman à chlef la première fois qu'elle est venue elle avait 6 mois
elle est repartie elle est revenue à 4 ans elle est repartie elle est revenue à 19 ans
mes parents se parlent dans les 2 langues ils me parlent dans les 2 langues
ma première langue c'est le français après la langue arabe a pris
le dessus maintenant ça s'est rééquilibré je suis revenue hier
d'algérie il faisait trop chaud ça faisait 3 ans que j'y étais pas retournée

à marseille aussi j'ai de la famille à la castellane à consolat à la belle de mai
ici dans le quartier j'ai mes 2 grands-mères à chlef y'a un quartier entier
c'est que ma famille j'aimerais bien mettre ici tous les gens que j'aime à chlef
et à chlef tous les gens que j'aime ici je suis un peu déchirée là-bas
j'aime les paysages la campagne les poules les vaches les moutons

à vrai dire je préfère marseille à avignon mais j'aime aussi avignon
parce que avignon c'est ma ville je me sens bien à monclar

à la fin de chaque histoire il y a une nouvelle histoire moi
j'ai l'impression d'avoir grandi trop vite

on se déteste parce qu'on parle pas la même langue
des fois on peut se détester à cause des attentats
on se connaît mal quand on parle pas la même langue
les rivières les mers c'est des frontières en vérité
j'aimerais aller en chine j'aimerais aller à pékin
je vais à mayotte de temps en temps mais ça fait loin

il y a des ponts j'ai déjà passé la frontière de la belgique
et la frontière de l'angleterre ma famille elle est en france
en angleterre en algérie je suis né à avignon à urbain 5
ceux du côté de ma mère vivent en angleterre ma mère elle est originaire de
là mais je parle pas beaucoup avec elle en classe j'ai pas de bonnes notes
en anglais par contre quand je parle avec les anglais j'y arrive
en jouant à *clash of clan* là je me débrouille bien

je suis allé une fois en angleterre mais c'est cher il vaut mieux vivre
à dunkerque comme ça on peut travailler la journée rentrer le soir
du côté de mon beau-père j'ai de la famille en algérie j'aime bien avignon
mais je préfère marseille parce qu'à marseille
il y a un métro avec des roues de voiture

le premier jour quand on rentre à l'école on franchit une frontière
après c'est la vie de tous les jours plus tard j'aimerais bien

franchir les frontières de l'amérique aller un peu partout

des fois les frontières c'est entre les copains quand on se dispute
ça nous bloque on recule au lieu d'avancer

avec les adultes la frontière c'est les secrets qu'ils gardent
par exemple quand quelqu'un meurt et aussi quand
ils veulent pas dire le cadeau qu'ils vont nous faire
l'âge la mémoire les mots qu'on connaît pas
c'est ça leur frontière

une dispute ça pourrait nous séparer
je suis né à mayotte je suis là depuis 3 mois je suis en 4ème
j'ai quitté ma petite sœur mon petit frère mon père je suis parti avec ma mère
mon autre petit frère lui il est à marseille chez mon oncle
mon rêve c'était de voir la tour eiffel en vrai mais le voyage était très très
long quand on est arrivés à paris c'est une amie de ma mère qui nous a
amenés jusqu'au métro pour aller à la gare prendre le train j'ai pas pu
voir la tour eiffel je voudrais retourner à paris pour la voir
arrivés à marseille on est restés une journée j'étais crevé
complétement crevé ensuite on est partis en voiture chez ma tante
la sœur de maman ici à monclar en attendant de trouver un logement

ça me fait mal d'avoir laissé les jumeaux le 16 ils ont eu 9 ans
pour l'instant je me suis pas encore fait de copains y en a qui
se moquent parce que pour mon âge je suis petit de taille
le problème c'est que là-bas y avait trop de voyous par exemple si
t'étais de la ville qui s'appelle cavani les rivaux ceux de m'gombani
ils venaient ils te massacraient c'est pour ça que ma mère
elle a dit qu'il fallait partir je suis un peu inquiet pour mon père
mon frère et ma sœur ceux qui sont restés

ici c'est calme on cherche une maison si on trouve pas on ira à marseille
ou à paris je préférerais vivre dans une ville calme

une ville paisible comme avignon

la langue française ici elle coule dans les veines les gens qui habitent loin
ils se disent on sait pas bien parler il faut qu'on apprenne à parler bien
les gens ici se rendent pas compte que ça coule dans leurs veines

j'aimerais faire médecine si j'y arrive pas je ferai l'armée
à mayotte je relisais mes cahiers la nuit le matin je me levais
à 5 heures pour réviser un peu j'aimais pas l'école coranique
mais ce qui est bien c'est que j'ai appris à lire l'arabe cette année entre
l'espagnol et l'arabe j'ai choisi l'espagnol pour connaître une nouvelle langue

en ce moment j'ai souvent mal à la tête le bruit me donne mal à la tête quand j'étais à mayotte les classes de 6ème portaient des noms de fleurs les 5ème des noms d'auteurs les 4ème je sais plus les 3ème des noms de capitales européennes vu que j'étais en 5ème rousseau j'ai cherché le nom sur internet j'ai lu plein de choses sur rousseau sur l'éducation des enfants je sais même que son prénom c'était jean-jacques

abdelsam michel-françois michel najat
rabiâa leïla ensar mireille souhail
odile chloé samira boumedienne lucas
najat s nadia hayat nasser

kassym 4 ans samaar 7 ans kaïna 7 ans et demi fakri 9 ans et demi

11 juillet 16 12 juillet 16 26 juillet 16 27 juillet 16

granges d'orel *champfleury* *granges d'orel* *champfleury*
monclar *monclar*

fin de matinée *fin d'après-midi* *fin de journée*
frédérique guétat-liviani octobre 16 saint-ruf

contours and conditions of but it's a long way

1. What are the contours of **but it's a long way**?

2. The text closes with the name of Jean-Jacques Rousseau. Then a recitative of the names of people whose words are transcribed. What importance does this nominal end-point hold for the text? And its proximity to the names of people who were approached?

3. What becomes of the author in proximity to these transcriptions?

4. The condition of **but it's a long way** is an accumulation of distances. The condition of speech is that of a proximity. What is the sense of this abyss? Is it an abyss?

5. **but it's a long way** is built in the breaches of walls, borders and barbed wire. The text seems to offer itself in counterpoint as a respiration. What is this architecture, for you, transcribing, for the body that attunes itself to this movement? What emotion?

What are the contours of **but it's a long way**?

but it's a long way was written following a series of encounters with the inhabitants of three extra-mural projects in Avignon. The encounters took place in the month of July 2016 while, intra-murally, as is the case every year, the Festival d'Avignon was underway. Avignon is a small city, the distances are short. Yet the ramparts encircling the old city seem impassable. Festival goers remain inside. The inhabitants live on the outside. A long time ago, I studied, inside. Later, I earned a living, outside. An association called l'Antre Lieux invited us, Sarah Kéryna and myself, to cross this demarcation line, at the height of summer. Liliane Giraudon joined us in the fall.

For each encounter, the same protocol: a table, two chairs, facing one another, a big ledger and several tracts mentioning the border as well as its crossing.

The whole thing set up at the foot of the residences.

Three different neighbourhoods, nonetheless similar, in the infinity of the forbidden space.

The encounters happen in the open air but the space is closed, there is silence around.

The contours cannot be written. They draw themselves, back-lit, against invisible screens.

Women, men, children, come to sit at my table. They speak, I write their words.

Always by hand, no recourse to some machine or other.

The slackening of the contour, its near effacement, this is the only cost at which the held views of the city can be transgressed.

The singular word then rises to the surface.

The contour of the words on the ledger render visible the time spent together, at the same table.

Visible are both the trembling bodies and time trembling.

The text closes on the name of Jean-Jacques Rousseau. Followed by a recitative of the names of people whose words are transcribed. What importance does this nominal outcome hold for the text? And its proximity to the names of those people who were approached?

Transcription is a gesture. A gesture does not have the finality of an action. By reproducing them, through writing, the names heard are transfigured. Without a portend as to their becoming. A name is heavy to carry. To transcribe it is to return to it a bit of its lightness. The same is true of the names of the projects. Often nicknamed rather than named, and subjected to the same fate as their inhabitants. They are not cited, they are spoken about. Thus, I copied out several formulas in the press. Common formulas for the inventory of the unnamed:

people of the projects, sensitive areas, disadvantaged people, undocumented, ineligible, clandestine, refugees, single-parent families, first-time offender, traffickers, job applicants, women in a precarious situation, radicalized youth, with suicidal tencencies, on parole, RSA beneficiaries, unregistered at the Pôle emploi*, beneficiaries of the social minimum, drug addicted, protective residency, on the wait-list for social housing...*

They are spoken of in the third person. A person who is absolutely non-existent, absent to herself or himself, outside of history without a past without a future. That society carries, like a weight. A weight is not named, it is only measurable. That is why I wanted to convoke all the heard voices. To call them by their own names, mixed with Rousseau's, the only author whose name was cited during these meetings. Rousseau, whose errancy accompanies that of the little boy from the Comoros, not long ago.

What becomes of the author alongside these transcriptions?

The author —it seems to me— is not erased. The author is allied to the others, through a silent pact. The words are not erased either. As soon as they are written down, they are displaced, organize themselves and dislocate. Ties are created, that had hitherto been discerned. It is certainly in the blanks, the spaces, that I am most present. I hold myself there because those who are speaking, speak to us so rarely. We who are saturated with discourses, information, commentaries. Placing space betwen their words is a way of keeping quiet, in order that they better be heard. To make things and facts be heard, to be the author of restitution. All the people encountered continually hesitated. They sometimes hesitated because of the French language, which was foreign to them. They hesitated at other times, not finding the word that suited them. They hesitated, carried away by their narrative, not knowing anymore where they were with it. Their hesitations suspended speaking and the body as well, in an unstable equilibrium on the office chairs we had placed on the dry lawn. The sentences were split wide open. I tried to retrieve these cracks in writing, in the rhythm of the line. Those who came to sit across from me were all so different, in terms of their age, their sex, their origins. But errancy was the thread that connected all of their narratives. I wanted to hold on to the evidence of this by not cutting that thread, by allowing it to spread out from one end to the other, like a streak. That is what I attempted to do, to retrieve the substance of interrupted speech, through the proliferation of cesurae. I remained there, suspended from the gesture of writing.

The condition of but it's a long way is an accumulation of distances. The condition of its speaking is that of a proximity. What is the sense of this abyss? Is it an abyss?

Élisée Reclus while drawing atlases would say: "one must definitively gain consciousness of our human solidarity, forming one body with the planet itself."

The distances have been travelled. They have imprinted themselves in the bodies that have come to a halt. All those who came to sit at my table, had travelled some road, a long road. That road is in them, in their bodies, in the body of their lineage. All of them are at a distance from a history, a family, a place, a memory. They have distanced themselves. *but it's a long way* is a halt. One must mark a pause, stop moving, to be able to speak of it, of the distance. To retrieve the inertia, resist walking, sit down a while. I don't think there is an abyss between the distance travelled and the words deposited there. The abyss is bottomless, one is voided there. *but it's a long way* is a receptacle for speech, the one receives, the other sets itself down. It's a hollow, a roundness that is in sharp contrast with the angular architecture of the projects encircling the table. It's like an inner hole that we are digging, without recourse to any tools other than language. Here, geographic distance is abolished.

but it's a long way is built inside the breaches of walls, borders and barbed wire. The text seems to offer itself as a counterpoint, as a respiration. What is this architecture, for you, transcribing, for the body attuned to this movement? What emotion?

> *"these lines speak [...] of a passage over that which is read to the point of bleeding, to the point of the wound."*
>
> —Jacques Derrida*

Writing is an enterprise that tends to unwall. It enters into the walls, turns them over, they become the support for that which they had a mission to prevent.

Behind those, there is the multitude of lives. Through the gaps of writing, one discerns the layering of voices that emerge from them. In the entanglement, they rise but one doesn't cover over the others. They nest in one another, contradict, and question one another. The walls against which they have collided, the wire on which some have been torn, have left holes, gashes. The leafing of voices has allowed words to migrate, from one narrative to another.

They escape in the line spacing, one retrieves them later, articulated and transformed, in other mouths. The voices of *but it's a long way* incorporate silence. Emotion is not pronounced. Sometimes the blanks are inscribed as a sign of mourning, sometimes as a sign of the unheard of. They are never ornaments. They are not intermissions, there are no acts. There are gestures. Speaking is a gesture similar to the one that stitches the snag. It is in order to exceed the impossibility of speaking that one enters inside. By following the passage where the walls that formed one body have erroded. At that precise place where the human meets the other.

The repetition of flight plunges into shock. The space of the text is that archive. In the incessant movement between here and elsewhere, the words exchanged become the auxiliary of displacement. Writing is a way to give substance to those whose lives were spoliated.

Well before their arrival in the world.

RSA: Revenue de solidarité active/Active solidarity income: The purpose of the RSA is to "guarantee its receipients sufficient means for living, in order to combat poverty, encourage the exercise of or return to professional activity and assist in the social integration of recipients" (Law no2008-1249 of December 1, 2008). From information provided by the Insee (National Institute of Statistics and Economic Studies), France.

Pôle emploi: employment agency. This French governmental agency has as its mission to register unemployed people, provide opportunities to find work, and provide financial aid.

Quote from Jacques Derrida on p. 89 tr. Joshua Wilner and Thomas Dutoit, modified.

Born in Grenoble in 1963, FRÉDÉRIQUE GUÉTAT-LIVIANI makes installations that speak of languages, and writes texts that she builds like images. A founding member of the artists' collective Intime Conviction (1988–94), she is now the publisher of Fidel Anthelme x. The author of several collections of poetry, she is of the caste neither of poets nor of artists. Instead, she inhabits a space in-between. She lives in Marseille.

NATHANAËL is the author of more than thirty books written in English or in French and published in the United States, Québec and France. Her translations include works by Catherine Mavrikakis, Édouard Glissant, Hervé Guibert, Reginald Gibbons, and Hilda Hilst (the latter in collaboration with Rachel Gontijo Araújo). Nathanaël lives in Chicago.

NIGHTBOAT BOOKS

Nightboat Books, a nonprofit organization, seeks to develop audiences for writers whose work resists convention and transcends boundaries. We publish books rich with poignancy, intelligence, and risk. Please visit nightboat.org to learn more about us and how you can support our future publications.

The following individuals have supported the publication of this book. We thank them for their generosity and commitment to the mission of Nightboat Books:

Elizabeth Motika
Benjamin Taylor

In addition, this book has been made possible, in part, by a grant from the National Endowment for the Arts and the New York State Council on the Arts Literature Program.

Traverser *passer* franchir essayer **rallier**

rejoindre venir se rendre *se faufiler* **s'effacer**

transiter *changer* **disparaître** ***marcher*** **s'en aller**

se glisser **fuir** laisser *quitter* tenter

Traverser *passer* franchir essayer **rallier**

rejoindre venir se rendre *se faufiler* **s'effacer**

transiter *changer* **disparaître** ***marcher*** **s'en aller**

se glisser **fuir** laisser *quitter* tenter

La lisière **au bord** ***le mur***

la séparation **au bout** la frontière la ligne de démarcation

à la fin la limite **la bordure**

de l'autre côté *à l'extrémité*

La lisière **au bord** ***le mur***

la séparation **au bout** la frontière la ligne de démarcation

à la fin la limite **la bordure**

de l'autre côté *à l'extrémité*